PALACE WITHIN

Exploring Teresa of Avila's Interior Castle

A WORKBOOK

Gillian T. W. Ahlgren

Palace Within: Exploring Teresa of Avila's *Interior Castle* (A Workbook)
Copyright © 2025 by Gillian T. W. Ahlgren
Published by VITALITY buzz, bliss + books LLC
vitalitybuzz.org

VITALITY buzz, bliss + books LLC publishes original creations to grow the mission of VITALITY Cincinnati Inc, a 501(c)3 education-based nonprofit sharing holistic self-care from neighborhood to neighborhood, person to person, and breath by breath since 2010.

Every effort has been made to give credit to other people's original ideas through the text. If you feel something should be credited to someone and is not, please get in touch through our website and every effort will be made to correct this text for future printings. Thank you!

Julie Lucas of withinwonder.com created the cover and interior artwork. Kathy Kohl contributed her artistic vision to the Contemplative Wisdom for Today logo. Thank you to Nancy Bradley and Barbara Donne for proofreading with such care!

We invite you to honor your mind, your body, your whole self. Do only what you know to be right for you. While the invitations offered here in this book, on our websites and social media, and in our classes are geared to be gentle and easily modified by the participant to fit the participants' needs, please consult your medical doctor or health professional before undertaking any practices.

ISBN: 978-1-954688-37-7

Contemplative
Wisdom for
Today

Translating the wisdom of the Christian mystical tradition for
our challenging times from visionary voices like:

Francis and Clare of Assisi,
Teresa of Avila,
Julian of Norwich,
Ignatius Loyola,
and many more.

Written by one of the leading scholars of the Christian mystical
tradition, Dr. Gillian Ahlgren, author of

Teresa of Avila and the Politics of Sanctity,

Entering Teresa of Avila's Interior Castle: A Reader's Companion,

Enkindling Love: The Legacy of Teresa of Avila and John of the Cross,

The Tenderness of God: Reclaiming Our Humanity,

Spiritual Exercises for the 21st Century: A Workbook

For Julie Murray,
with affection and gratitude

in gratitude

to the VATRONS
who breathed life into this book
by pre-ordering their copy

Alice & James Ahlgren, William Amrhein, Wesley Behrman, Nancy Bradley, Catherine Clark, Pamela Cobey, Barbara Donne, Ernest Drott, Miguel Gallardo, Fred Hatchet, Beth Lake, Julie Murray, Notre Dame Retreat House (Canandaigua, NY), Mary Virginia Quinn, Maureen Roderick, Stacey Sands, Marilyn Schleyer, Aida Segura, Brian Shircliff, James Siegel, Tracy Stephens, Mary Zeller

CONTENTS

The Interior Castle

FIRST DWELLING PLACES
39

SECOND DWELLING PLACES
53

THIRD DWELLING PLACES
63

FOURTH DWELLING PLACES
69

FIFTH DWELLING PLACES
75

SIXTH DWELLING PLACES
83

SEVENTH DWELLING PLACES
91

Committing Yourself to Ongoing Growth
97

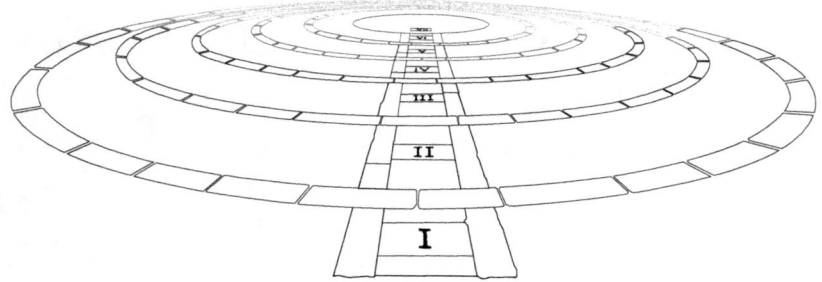

About This Book

What does a woman born over 500 years ago have to teach us today? Teresa of Avila's wisdom, about God, life and the challenges of being human, speak to us across the ages, with a refreshing practicality, wit and candor that we do not always associate with sanctity. Teresa's deep honesty, her humor, her humility, and her radical self-disclosure have made her writings accessible to generations of readers, especially those seeking authentic relationship with God. Her words stimulate both a deep introspection and a hopeful sense that no genuine thirst for God comes solely from us, but has actually been implanted in us by the One who loves us into life.

Teresa has been teacher, mentor and friend to me over a lifetime of growth as a scholar, teacher and contemplative. After fifteen years of teaching Teresa in the classroom and dedicating myself to the contemplative way, I published a small book, *Entering Teresa of Avila's Interior Castle: A Reader's Companion* (Paulist Press, 2005), in which I outlined, stage by stage, the theological-spiritual synthesis that Teresa captures so brilliantly in her *Interior Castle*. After that book was published, people began asking me why I had not written more practically about the mystical way Teresa lived. Readers wanted to know how they, too, could advance spiritually along the path Teresa outlines.

This book is a much-delayed response to those readers, as well as a synthesis of some of what I have learned through my own life, my ongoing teaching, and twenty more years of pastoral work. Some might say I am a slow learner, and I would readily admit that. But, like many people in the 21st century, my life has also been beset by twists and turns that I could never have predicted and which demanded and required their due attention. Each twist and turn since 2005, however, has shown me the practical relevance of Teresa's abiding wisdom, in ways that I might not have been able to appreciate until later in my life. I am now nearly the same age as Teresa was when she wrote *The Interior Castle*, and I am more convinced than ever of its capacity to change lives. Teresa's wisdom reveals itself with time and experience, particularly if we dedicate ourselves to ongoing learning and growth.

Palace Within is not comprehensive; rather, it is truly a workbook, meant to allow you many paths for reflection, self-improvement, and, above all, deepening relationship with God. The exercises in the workbook correlate to each of the seven dwelling places of *The Interior Castle*, and they will give you points of entry to explore the content in each dwelling place. But because the seven dwelling places represent stages in a cumulative process of transformative growth, the material in the fourth dwelling places and beyond may remain opaque and theoretical if you are not growing and progressing with each stage.

Teresa herself says repeatedly that spiritual growth is what happens in the intimate space between us and God, a space that is enhanced when we have good spiritual companions to help us engage and stay faithful to the growth process. As you move through these exercises, you should have trusted friends in God with whom to share what you are noticing. You should also use this book in tandem with Teresa's *Interior Castle* (I recommend the English translation of Kieran Kavanaugh and Otilio Rodriguez) and *Entering Teresa of Avila's Interior Castle: A Reader's Companion*. Although I have left some space in this book for your reflections, you might like more space in your own journal or notebook.

All translations of passages of *The Interior Castle* and Teresa's other works used in this workbook are my own and have been newly translated for this work.

Gillian T. W. Ahlgren

Who was Teresa of Avila?

Teresa of Avila was a vibrant woman, deeply committed to being close to God and known for her vivacity, her love of life, and her ability to draw people out in conversation and make an impact on their thinking. Her tenacious commitment to learning about God and cultivating relationship with God is matched only by her desire to make God accessible to others and encourage them to "taste and see" God's goodness and be changed.

Her life (1515-1582) spans some of the most turbulent years of Christian history—times of dramatic change in the European landscape—and the circumstances of her early life reflect that. Thirty years before she was even born, her grandfather was sentenced by the Inquisitional Tribunal of Toledo to public humiliation for being a Jewish convert to Christianity. To escape the stigma of this, he relocated his family from Toledo to Avila. Decades later, his sons (Teresa's father Alonso and her uncles) spent many years and much money on documents that rewrote their genealogy, giving them "pure blood"—a phrase used in sixteenth-century Spain to indicate that a family was free from Jewish origin. In the sixteenth century, demonstrating "purity of blood" was necessary for public service, access to legal proceedings in the civil courts, and even entry into many religious orders. Without the forged documents, descendants of converts to Christianity, like Teresa and her siblings, could not enter monasteries or convents.

Teresa was just four years old in 1519, when Martin Luther was excommunicated and the Reformation began tearing its way through Europe, spurring religious violence across the continent. In Spain, the response to the emerging Protestant movement was swift, as a deep suspicion of those seeking a life of spiritual depth and interiority took hold. By 1525, when Teresa was just ten years old, Spanish inquisitors' harsh treatment of *alumbrados* or "'falsely illuminated' people" had driven Ignatius Loyola from Spain altogether.

In 1528, when Teresa was 13 years old, her mother died. Her older sister married soon afterward, and there was no female presence left in the family home—no one to give Teresa advice or counsel, no one to insist on chaperones and proper conduct. Her father sent her to the Augustinian convent of Nuestra Señora de la Gracia as a boarding student. Teresa had mixed feelings about convent life, but in the end, she entered the Carmelite convent of the Encarnación in 1535, at the age of 20.

The Encarnación was a large convent of nearly 200 women, and it was a struggle to feed and support all of them. Wealthier nuns were encouraged to take their main meal back in their family homes, family members visited and brought gifts, and there was no real sense of enclosure. At first, Teresa seemed happy to take advantage of the lax standards. But she struggled with physical illness in her early years of convent life and nearly died. In *The Book of Her Life,* Teresa describes regaining consciousness after a coma and realizing, to her shock, that the sisters had already prepared her body for last rites and burial. During the year that she spent recovering from that illness in the home of her uncle, the bed-ridden young woman discovered her voracious appetite for learning about God. Who would teach her? Where could she go to learn?

University education was denied to women. And Teresa had run through the convent library. Poring through her uncle's collection of classic spiritual texts, Teresa sought to learn all of the techniques of what was then called "mental prayer."

Spanish translations of many such prayer manuals had been commissioned by the Franciscan reformer Francisco Jimenez de Cisneros, confessor to Queen Isabella during the years of spiritual revival prior to the Protestant Reformation. Teresa eagerly read all the books she could get her hands on: Francisco de Osuna's *Third Spiritual Alphabet*, Bernardino de Laredo's *Ascent of Mount Sion*, Augustine's *Confessions*, Catherine of Siena's *Dialogue*. In fact, although she was self-educated, Teresa's integration of Christianity's medieval spiritual and theological currents surpassed many of her male peers.

But it was not until the Jesuits arrived in Avila in 1553 and took her through Ignatius Loyola's Spiritual Exercises that Teresa learned a dialogical method of meditative prayer that ignited her relationship with God and slowly led her to become a spiritual teacher in her own right. As Teresa sought herself to live more deeply toward an empowering partnership with God, she became convinced that genuine and active collaboration with God was the vocation of each and every Christian. She dedicated herself both to creating the spaces for engaging deepening relationship with God and to teaching people how to grow into genuine collaboration with the One who asks just three things of us: to act justly, to love tenderly, and to walk humbly together with our God. (Micah 6:8)

For a woman in sixteenth-century Spain, especially after the publication of the Valdés Index of Prohibited Books in 1559, this was a challenge, indeed. The Valdés Index forbade reading scripture or any scriptural commentary in any language other than Latin. It also prohibited books written by some of the more important spiritual authors of Teresa's day, including Juan de Avila and Luis de Granada, with whom Teresa consulted about mental prayer. The Valdés Index communicated in very real terms an institutional suspicion of mental prayer that had significant implications for Teresa.

First, as a woman lacking theological education, Teresa would never have the authority to teach and was vulnerable to challenges by male contemporaries who were concerned that her experiences of God might not be authentic. Second, her evolving vision of reform within the Carmelite order was predicated upon a corps of informed, prayerful women. Yet the Index now banned some of the books Teresa and her sisters needed to sustain their spiritual growth. Deprived of them, how would women entering the contemplative life be able to learn mental prayer and live out their religious vocation?

The appearance of the Valdés Index was significant enough to Teresa for her to go to God with her lament. As she tells us in her *Life:*

> "When many books in the vernacular were taken away, so that they would not be read, I was very sorry, because it helped me to read them, and now I couldn't, since they were only available in Latin. But God said to me: 'Do not be troubled. I will give you a living book.'" (See *The Book of Her Life*, 26:6.)

The implication was two-fold: Teresa's direct relationship with God would give her all the theological education she would need, and, out of that experience, through her, God would teach those around her. As I argued in *Teresa of Avila and the Politics of Sanctity* many years ago, it was the challenge of the Valdés Index of Prohibited Books that cemented Teresa's vocation as a mystical theologian and teacher.

Over the course of her life, Teresa would write four major works—*The Book of Her Life*, a chronicling of her experiences of God over the first five decades of her life; *The Way of Perfection*, a basic manual of prayer for the sisters under her care; *The Book of Foundations*, an account of her activities as the reformer of the Carmelite order; and her masterpiece, *The Interior Castle*—

as well as many other works, including brief accounts of her spiritual life (*Relations*), poetry, monastic documents and letters (over 450 of them extant).

In 1562 Teresa founded the reformed Carmelite convent of San José in Avila, which became the first of many communities dedicated to cultivating contemplative prayer and engaging prayer on behalf of a troubled world. This very specific vocation gave women a clear and relevant role in the larger context of Catholic reform. Although the strictures of the Council of Trent were pushing women away from the church's apostolic orientation, Teresa's discalced Carmelite convents were a breath of fresh air for women who sought to respond to the invitation of God to friendship, intimacy, and intercessory prayer for a needy world. Teresa's reform quickly spread throughout Spain: San José in Avila was soon followed by foundations in Medina del Campo (1567), Malagón (1568) and Valladolid (1568), where she successfully recruited John of the Cross and arranged for the subsequent male foundation at Duruelo in 1568, male and female foundations in Pastrana (1569), and female foundations in Salamanca (1570) and Alba (1571).

When Teresa found herself unexpectedly named prioress at her original (and subsequently unreformed) convent of the Encarnación in 1571, the intensity of foundation activity slowed. Being prioress of this large community was, in many ways, simply a new manifestation of her reforming work. In the temporary respite from founding new convents, Teresa was able to work on developing the contemplative vocations of women who could then be relocated to join discalced convents throughout Castile.

As the administrator of a growing reform movement, Teresa used her formidable energy to produce and provide resources that wound ensure the stability and longevity, not only of the Discalced Carmelite order but of the contemplative practices that gave it *gravitas.* One of her first acts as prioress of the Encarnación was to summon her first male collaborator, the famous John of the Cross, to serve as the spiritual director of the community. This strategic move effectively turned the city of Avila into a kind of spiritual academy, training women in the mystical life and then sending them forth across the whole of Spain to dot the map with small epicenters of profound spiritual energy.

During the five years that John of the Cross lived in Avila (1572 to 1577), Teresa and John's powerful alliance contributed centrally to the larger Catholic reform movement. Knowing that John could manage the spiritual life of the sisters in Avila, Teresa returned to founding convents—in Segovia (1574), Beas (1575), Seville (1575), Caravaca (1576), Toledo (1579), Palencia (1580), Villanueva de la Jara (1580), Soria (1581), Burgos (1582) and Granada (1582), deploying people to go in her stead when she herself was unable. In total, it is estimated that Teresa traversed approximately 7500 kilometers, in a challenging combination of methods of transportation, from coaches to mules, over rutted dirt roads and in weather conditions of all kinds.

Teresa's vocation had two complementary facets, reformer and writer. Her work as a writer of reflections on the mystical life was an integral part of her reform; both facets of this double vocation awakened significant resistance even as they contributed substantively to the Catholic Reformation. Teresa was challenged by the Spanish Inquisition in two significant ways during her lifetime, and a case against her was opened posthumously after the publication of her *Complete Works* in 1588. You can read a far more detailed account of these challenges in *Teresa of Avila and the Politics of Sanctity*, but it is worth noting here that Teresa's problems with the Inquisition were directly responsible for her decision to write *The Interior Castle*.

In 1575 the Valladolid tribunal of the Spanish Inquisition ordered a theological review of Teresa's *Book of Her Life*. Although the censor, Domingo Báñez, knew Teresa personally and could vouch for her sincerity as a person, he expressed discomfort that the book circulate, since it contained "many revelations and visions, which should always be feared, especially in women, who are more likely to believe they come from God and to see holiness in them." As a result of this assessment, the original manuscript of Teresa's *Life* was held by the inquisitional tribunal, and Teresa was not able, during her lifetime, to get it back.

After her death, Teresa's colleague and confessor Jerónimo Gracián recounted their conversation in late 1576, shortly after Teresa had successfully defended the authenticity of her spiritual experiences before inquisitors from the tribunal of Seville:

Being her confessor and speaking with her once in Toledo about many things concerning her spirit, she said to me: "Oh, how well that point is written in the book of my life, which the Inquisition has!" And I said to her: "Well, since we can't recover it, write down what you remember, and other things, and write another book, and explain the basic doctrine without identifying the person who has experienced what you say there...."

The resulting treatise, Teresa's *Interior Castle*, is not a re-write of her *Life*, but is instead a dense and mature theological piece. Its careful defense of mystical prayer, visions, rapture and the doctrine of union with God can only be viewed as a bold response to inquisitional suspicion of mental prayer and "false mystics." All-too-keenly aware of both the internal and external obstacles faced by those dedicated to contemplation and the search for God, Teresa wrote the *Interior Castle* to offer readers a compass for their theological and spiritual journey.

By opening up for others the reality of deep and direct relationship with God, Teresa changed the face of Christian spirituality. Not only does she outline the mechanics of how this relationship deepens, she reveals the inner life of a genuine partnership with God, forged moment by moment, day by day, like every real relationship, which is always a work in progress and is constantly changing us insofar as we let it. Teresa epitomizes the transforming pedagogy of God. By allowing God to reveal Godself to her in ever new ways, Teresa models the relational process as a way of daily life.

In 1970, Teresa was named a doctor of the Roman Catholic church and accorded the title, "Doctor of Prayer." While her teachings on prayer are certainly how Teresa draws people to God, that title may not capture all that she offers us today. If we tend to think of contemplative prayer as something reserved for those who have retired from the world or who dedicate themselves to silence, Teresa opens up a new way for us to approach God, beginning with her simple and basic definition of prayer as "nothing more than frequent conversation with One whom we know loves us"—a dialogical way of coming to know God until, gradually, we are so attuned to God's constant companionship that we live in communion with God in our world.

Teresa teaches lessons applicable to every sphere of our lives—whether that means our life of prayer, our lives as professionals, our service to the community, our commitment to family, or our task of prophetic discipleship as we work to make this world a home for all. In fact, Teresa's vision of life in partnership with God helps us to see that the so-called "spheres" of our lives (prayer, family, religious vocation, professional service) are ultimately one single sphere—a sphere in which we allow the love of God to work its way into our hearts, our homes, and our world. The theological vision of Teresa helps us to see that our lives are to be one long prayer, that prayer is life and life is to be prayer, no matter what our circumstances, roles or vocations.

Teresa did not set out to become a theologian or a spiritual teacher. She set out to be faithful to the ongoing invitation to deepening life with God. And as God's self-revelation gave her a new sense of purpose, she followed her vocation to contemplative prayer through its logical stages, teaching and writing spiritual classics that have stood the test of time. Teresa had many reasons to write, not the least of which were "to answer questions about prayer" (See *Interior Castle*, Prologue, par. 4) and to help readers to "be dissolved in praises of the great God who created the soul in God's own image and likeness." (See *Interior Castle*, Epilogue, par. 3)

When we place her mystical synthesis in the context of the Valdés Index of Prohibited Books and her investigation by the Spanish Inquisition in Seville, Teresa's courage, ingenuity, and real brilliance as a writer becomes increasingly clear. One of Teresa's favorite passages from the Psalms was 89:1: "I will sing forever of God's mercy and loving kindness." This pledge was, truly, the core prayer of Teresa's life: to bear constant witness to the love of God in ways that allowed people to experience that love more completely and fully in their own lives.

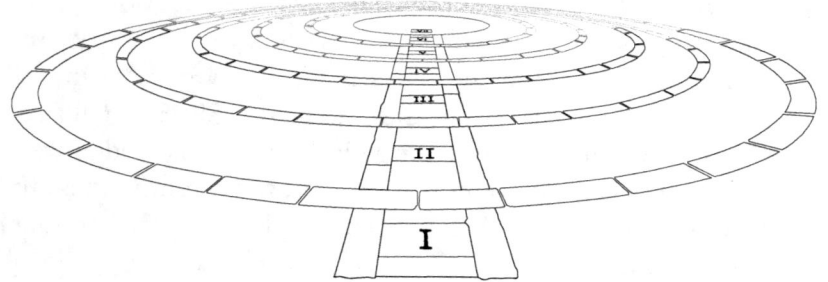

Some Features of Teresian Prayer

The backbone of Teresian spirituality is contemplative prayer. For Teresa, prayer was a practice that developed and evolved as her relationship with God deepened and matured. Informed by the many books about God and prayer circulating in Spain prior to the Valdés Index of Prohibited Books as well as her exposure to Ignatian spirituality and the Spiritual Exercises, Teresa had a variety of spiritual tools and experiential insights as she devoted herself more deeply to contemplative prayer and developed the discalced Carmelite tradition of spirituality. For Teresa prayer is not a technique but a practice of relational disposition to the presence of God that transforms and capacitates us over the course of our lives.

Growth is at the heart of prayer—growth in maturity, growth in generosity of spirit, growth in intimacy with God. In fact, Teresa seems to suggest that, as human beings, we are constantly advancing in relationship with God or losing ground, as she writes: "Whoever does not grow, shrinks." Time spent with God brings us insights that we can never reach on our own. We turn to God in prayer in order to be shown the ways that we and our world need to change and to be given the strength and courage to continue to strive toward goodness and purity of heart.

For Teresa prayer is always a relationship seeking constant depth and expansion. Prayer is relational activity: it encompasses all of the ways that we explore and cultivate relationships—with God, first and foremost, but also with ourselves and with others. The whole point of prayer is to enable our growth in love, a love that is expressed not only in words, but in how we live, moment to moment.

Prayer sensitizes us to the presence of God. It gives us eyes to see our world differently. Prayer motivates us not only to recognize and attend to God in the world around us, but also to be a part of God's desire for a better world. Most importantly, prayer enkindles love in us—a love that gives us fortitude, emboldening us to make choices toward the deepening of God's life, in us and in our world. Prayer encompasses both the context in which relationship with God develops and the practices that habituate us to that central relationship that gives life to us and our world.

As we become more accustomed to relationship with God and the practices that accompany that relationship, our human relationships gain a grounding that enables them and us to flourish. Because prayer is life-giving relationship, it is ultimately the key to growth, resilience and full human flourishing.

We need not be an expert in prayer to recognize its benefits in our lives, particularly if we are honest about our own personal limitations and vulnerabilities. Even our limited experiences of prayer teach us that, as we reach to God for help, consolation, guidance, or company, we grow in wisdom, insight, purpose, and even serenity. But Teresa can give us a way to become more systematic and deliberate about prayer and about the relational growth to which it invites us.

Although Teresa is known as a teacher of contemplative prayer, I believe that her insights into both prayer and personhood are applicable to all. As an educator and as a pastoral theologian, I often hear people say, "I don't really know how to pray!" or "I don't have the temperament for contemplation," as if prayer were for special people with the patience and dedication of saints. Nothing could be further from the truth. In fact, Teresa's own honesty about decades of struggle with prayer provides helpful, experiential counsel for all of us.

Teresa is sympathetic to the restlessness of the human mind, acknowledging that it routinely "flies about quickly," distracting us from greater absorption in God. When we find it difficult to concentrate or focus in prayer, she advises us to go gently, reminding us that "you cannot begin to recollect yourselves by force but only by gentleness, if your recollection is going to be continual." (*Interior Castle* II:1:10)

Teresa teaches us that prayer is as natural to us as life itself; it is not meant to be stiff or formal but conversational, colloquial, intimate and heartfelt. Teresa's basic style of prayer could best be described as "dialogical." What does this mean? She herself tells us, in her core, operational definition of prayer:

> "Prayer is nothing more than intimate conversation with a friend. It means taking time frequently to be alone with the One whom we know loves us." (Teresa, *Book of Her Life*, 8:5)

Just like with people, our conversations with God vary. Prayer captures the many ways that we approach God with familiarity, humility and openness to the possibility of some sort of exchange. "Dialogue" with God need not involve the hearing of particular words from God; here "dialogue" suggests a relational disposition in us: we go into prayer with openness to meet and be met. As we become more aware and spiritually sensitive to the presence of God and as we share more concretely our inner lives (hopes, dreams, concerns, fears, disappointments) with God, new forms of communication may emerge. This dialogical approach to prayer is a natural outgrowth of our openness to the possibility that we might discover, in God, our truest friend.

Familiarity with God does not imply that our prayer should be thoughtless, haphazard, or careless, as Teresa cautions:

> "A prayer in which a person is not aware of to whom she is speaking, what she is asking, who it is who is asking and of whom, I do not call prayer, however much the lips may

move.... Anyone who has the habit of saying whatever comes into one's head or whatever one has learned from saying at other times, in my opinion is not praying." (*Interior Castle* I:1:7)

What stands out here is Teresa's insistence on the *currency* of our encounters with God: we bring our intention and our current reality into our time with God, doing so in a thoughtful way that makes each moment with God unique. We will never be in the exact same space, internally or externally, in each moment of our lives, and we share from the specificity of that space with God as often as we can.

To put it another way, Teresa teaches that intentionality, personal presence, and thorough investment in the moment of encounter with God are the hallmarks of authentic prayer. She calls people into the mystery of direct engagement with the divine whenever and wherever they turn to prayer, and, as we engage God in the fullness of our being, we grow in self-possession and generous self-offering. Although we bring the whole of ourselves to prayer, prayer is never all about us. We bring to prayer what most concerns us, what draws our attention, what spins around in our heads as we fret about it; yet we come into God's presence lightly, clearing plenty of space for God to be with us. It is in this space of prayer that we begin to realize that we may be more, not just less, than what we think.

Prayer broadens our capacity at levels that encompass and surpass our cognitive abilities: the all-encompassing reality of prayer breaks down, integrates, and reconfigures how we see, know, feel and understand. It is not easy to speak about such a complex and ineffable process. Repeatedly, Teresa counsels us that we should not undergo transformative prayer alone and that we should seek out those who are more advanced in prayer, for counsel, support, and accompaniment.

Beginners in the process of colloquial prayer may well wonder: What is the subject matter of conversation with God? The answer is simple: anything and everything that is worthy of our time with God. In times of crisis, there are pressing matters in our lives that, because of their importance to us, take up much of our conversational space. But we should continually ask ourselves whether what we are bringing to God in prayer is the thing that will best advance and strengthen our relationship with God. If we take a moment, from a space of inner simplicity, to ask ourselves what we most need and want, that kind of directness can crystallize our focus and helpfully prepare for conversation.

It is also important to remember that conversation is mutually self-disclosive, not one-sided. On our part, this involves a willingness to consider and offer up the parts of ourselves that are most difficult, hidden, or unrealized; these are inner spaces where the relational reality of prayer can be most beneficial to us. In practical terms, this might take forms in which we consider some of the things that we have noticed about ourselves and never really understood, holding them up for deepening enlightenment. We might seek greater honesty about areas of our lives or our personhood where we have actively or passively avoided contact with God, allowing for greater awareness of where we have resisted depth in our relationship with God. As we sit with God in silence and loving attentiveness, receiving God with gratitude, hope and love, we might become aware of how much of ourselves we withhold from God. Such willingness to be shown the possibilities of deeper intimacy with God helps move the practice of colloquy into realms of growth that we can never touch on our own.

As the fundamental backbone of our relationship with God, prayer cannot be disembodied, disinterested conversation with an abstract entity "somewhere out there." The more of ourselves we invest in prayer, the more we begin to have a sense and feel for the One with whom we are in relationship. In my experience, the more dialogical that prayer becomes, the more sensory and more incarnate it becomes, generating new sensitivities and forms of conversation and connectedness as we give ourselves over more relationally to God.

These observations should make it clear that prayer is transformative. It changes us. The change is palpable, measured not only in terms of the personal growth, maturity, discretion, and wisdom that we acquire, but also in our loving disposition, concern and desire for the well-being of others. Prayer gives us sensitivities to see what is wrong, unjust, demoralizing, and unworthy of us and of one another. Prayer gives us the courage to denounce these injustices and the wisdom to know how to change the things that need changing, in us and in our world.

As Teresa describes in *The Interior Castle*, prayer increases our capacity to love. Once we have decided to put God's will before our own, prayer shows us that God's will is that we grow toward a partnership with God that gives us life and possibility. Ultimately, that partnership brings light to the world and asks us to collaborate with God in the work of making the world a place where God would feel at home.

True transformation derives from relationship, and intimacy is a critical part of mature relationship. As Teresa shows us, relationship with God constantly draws us out of the smallness of ourselves, expanding our personhood and creating a habit of flourishing relationality. Prayer is (and ought to be) the incubating space for the incarnation of God in the human community. It is not a space where we attempt to influence, cajole, or make demands on God. It is a relational process that happens partly because of our self-dedication but mostly because of our openness to discover what God wants, from us, for us and with us. Prayer requires us to continually re-envision ourselves and our world, stimulating a prophetic imagination and providing us with new aspirations, for ourselves and for the human community.

Gillian T. W. Ahlgren

Prayer asks us to prioritize human growth, personally and communally, over any other thing. Communities of prayer, as Teresa envisioned and created them, embody love, value wisdom over piety, and recognize that such wisdom is creative and practical, able to resist and provide graced alternatives to abuse, degradation, violence and indignity. Prayer empowers us to be "wise as serpents and gentle as doves" (Matthew 10:16) and is the avenue for strength in a world that often resists the hopeful grace of human tenderness.

Transformation, as a concept or as a practical reality, may seem amorphous or haphazard, but in *The Interior Castle* Teresa provides a very clear progression of steps. We could consider these steps to be developmental milestones, involving the will, the affect, the intellect, and a dedication to relational practices capable of transforming our current reality.

Ultimately, prayer is life. As prayer becomes life and our life becomes a long, sustained prayer, prayer is the trustworthy relational context in which we grow into our identity as God's beloved and become ourselves.

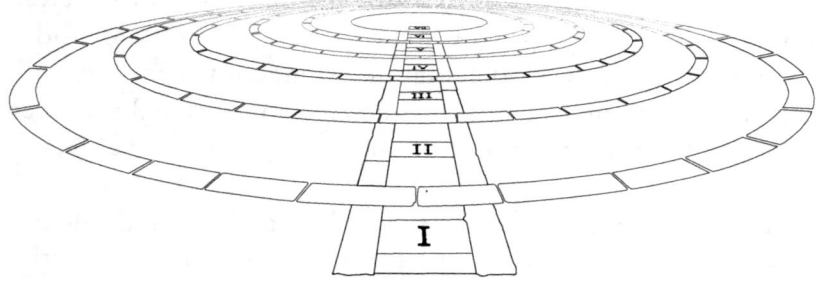

The Interior Castle:
A Basic Outline

The Interior Castle is a work of seven sections, each representing a stage in the progression of our growth toward union with God. The union accomplished in the seventh stage is neither a state nor is it static. Instead, we grow into an *ever-deepening collaborative partnership with God* that has been forged along the way and is, by that seventh stage, operative, in us and in the world around us. Teresa's teachings in *The Interior Castle* continually challenge and "correct" some of our notions of the mystical life: first and foremost, that union with God is something that some of us may receive after departing from this life, and second, that this union is something reached fleetingly in this life. In Teresa's experience (and thus in the language of *The Interior Castle*, her most mature spiritual and theological work), union with God is a functional partnership, one that is constantly active in the human community. In this sense, union with God happens both in us, as God comes alive within us, and around us, as God's presence is made manifest and shared in the human community.

Each stage in the progression of our journey toward union with God is a "dwelling place," which Teresa uses in the plural ("Dwelling Places"), replicating the "many rooms" in the house of God referred to in John 14:2. The sequential nature of these stages becomes immediately clear to the reader, because in each of the seven dwelling places there are certain things that people need to understand and integrate into their lives before they move onto the next stage.

The first three dwelling places are sometimes called the "moral dwelling places," because they involve behavior, choices, and commitments. The fourth dwelling places can be considered transitional, and the final three dwelling places are more properly called "mystical," because they represent transformation effected in us by God, with our consent and cooperation. Teresa herself calls the first three dwelling places "natural" and the final four "supernatural," in order to make this distinction.

Before we explore each of the dwelling places, here is a summary of the overarching movement, from one to the next:

FIRST DWELLING PLACES

How do we know who we are, what matters to us, and why we are here on this earth? We might start by recognizing that there is more to us than what the world acknowledges. There is a depth to our being, which Teresa would call our "soul." If that word seems too foreign to you, find one that captures our capacity, as humans and as persons in constant formation, to transcend limitation, to participate in creative activity, and to come into our truest, best self, as persons-in-relation to God and to others. There are many ways to capture this reality, and the work of the First Dwelling Places is simply to recognize that there is a path to something more than who we currently are. Relationship with the divine, in whom we have our origin, *is* that path. This stage involves considering and acknowledging the dignity of ourselves and our origins in something more than ourselves. The next two stages involve what we *do* in direct response to the recognition of our innate dignity—a dignity that our world and we ourselves do not always honor.

We can explore the reality of our innate dignity in two primary ways, affirmation and denial. We can reflect on how it has felt to fall short of our dignity, to participate in things that are not worthy of us, or to have our dignity denied, even denigrated by others. But the even more powerful way, for Teresa, is to behold our dignity in and through the purity and beauty of God in whose image we are created. Even when we find ourselves very far from the divine image, such a consideration gives us an illuminating vision of our potential and an appetite to explore who we can become.

SECOND DWELLING PLACES

The Second Dwelling Places is a space of more painful self-knowledge, as we become more aware of how often we have fallen short of our potential as human beings. In reviewing our lives and considering our current reality, we come to see how often we have turned away from what would have been better for us and have missed opportunities for growth in goodness. In the Second Dwelling Places we also take time to consider our lives as gifts and the extent to which we have been good stewards of the gifts we have been given. These considerations are not abstract, gratuitous, or designed to induce shame or guilt; they are done in order to awaken us to a deeper purpose and help us realize what we have to offer a needy world.

As we reflect on our own life histories and on the less savory characteristics of human beings (e.g., selfishness, greed, envy, arrogance, callousness, carelessness, recklessness, even violence and destruction), we understand and become sensitized to how we have been coopted into the "mess" that human beings have made of our world. As we come to terms with how we personally have fallen short, we may also become more aware of how others have fallen short in valuing and supporting us and our giftedness. All of these considerations remind us that life is a journey, and, for that journey, we need good companions— people who will help us grow into our capacity for goodness.

As human beings, we are meant to thrive. As we become more honest about that and more aware about how many obstacles there are along the way and how much unnecessary suffering is present in our world, we gain the hopeful realization that perhaps, working more constructively with God and with one another, it may not be too late to create a more meaningful life and have a positive impact on our world.

THIRD DWELLING PLACES

Roused and motivated in the Second Dwelling Places by all that we know we need to leave behind, we accomplish something in the Third Dwelling Places as we devote ourselves to the growth in virtue that leads to better and wiser life choices. Teresa speaks of the Third Dwelling Places as a space where we have overcome habits that are unhealthy, self-destructive, or immoral and have gained a certain peace of mind and conscience.

But there is still a long relational road ahead of us, and ridding ourselves of habits that keep us from freely choosing a good and godly life is only a necessary first step on the way to becoming a trustworthy friend of God. In fact, what is called for at this stage is an entirely new conception of what relationship with God is like: rather than being about what we believe and do, relationship with God involves depth of character, growth in wisdom and compassion, and a radical reorientation of our lives toward intimacy with God.

The second half of this stage involves choosing God as teacher and companion. We will not proceed further without committing ourselves to this friendship that gives new life and new possibility and asks us to align our vision, our goals, and our daily lives to learning what love is and what love does.

Gillian T.W. Ahlgren

FOURTH DWELLING PLACES

Teresa begins this stage of the journey toward union with God with a scriptural reference from Psalm 118:32: "when you have enlarged my heart," using this quote to describe the expansion of our personhood as we learn how to sustain deepening relationship with God. Our hearts are enlarged with affection, admiration, and deepening love for God, especially as we spend more time with God and allow God's self-revelation to surprise us.

As God's love invites and capacitates us to love more deeply, more compassionately, and more fully, a relational space for God is built within us. We receive our first direct tastes of God as we spend more time with God, and these tastes of God generate new interests, concerns and orientations in us. Our time with God reveals previously unknown interior depths, and our relationship with God proves to be a pathway leading toward a place in us that we cannot access by ourselves. Empowered by God's love, we find it less difficult to place our individual faculties—the will, the intellect, and the emotions—directly in the service of our relationship with God.

FIFTH DWELLING PLACES

Having been expanded within by encounters with God, our work in the Fifth Dwelling Places is to draw inward and come to know that relational space. Teresa speaks of a turtle being drawn into its shell and of a caterpillar building its cocoon, entering, and then becoming a butterfly. The space created within us through the process of expansion now becomes the location for a powerful transformation which helps us begin to appropriate a truly relational identity.

The experience of union with God at this stage is brief but more intense than we have ever known previously; Teresa describes it as felt "in the marrow of the bones" rather than at the surface. Here, our experience of prayer feels like a temporary absorption in God, where our normal cognitive abilities are temporarily diminished, and we experience the suspension of time as we begin to know something of the essence of God. Such experiences drive a true transformation through an organic process germane to the image of God in which we find our deepest origins. We acquire an identity-in-and-with-God, through a process that we cannot control but can gracefully grow into. Teresa likens this to the early days of a butterfly, which does not actually fly directly out of its cocoon. Instead, it learns movement as a new entity only after its wings have dried and it gains the use of them. In the Fifth Dwelling Places we have been so placed within the grandeur of God that we now possess tremendous desires and growing capacities to do good and to love deeply.

SIXTH DWELLING PLACES

The Sixth Dwelling Places, consisting of eleven chapters, contain the most complex and difficult material in *The Interior Castle*. In fact, this section is fully as long as the five dwelling places that have preceded it. In this section, Teresa describes the multiple ways that ongoing encounters with God prepare us for a functional partnership with God that will bear fruit in the Seventh Dwelling Places—such that, ultimately, our union with God is both a "resting place" and an empowered space of divinely-inspired action in the world around us. For this partnership to be actuated, we must be sensitized to the many ways that God wants to communicate things to us, wants to energize us, wants to inspire and ignite our capacity to be instruments of God's own love.

This capacitation takes multiple forms and is unique in each person. Teresa appreciates how partnership with God unfolds differently in all of us. For this reason, she includes as much detail as she can about how our partnership with God may be

Gillian T.W. Ahlgren

forged. When we take into consideration the suspicion and even disdain that some clerics had for women's moral and spiritual capacity, we can also read the material in this section as a strategic manual for the discernment of spirits, so that women could withstand withering criticism of their inner lives. When we think of the crucible of purification that some chemical processes require, we have an apt analogy for what we undergo in our final preparation for a partnership with God that will prove itself, time and again, despite potential pressure in a malicious world.

SEVENTH DWELLING PLACES

After the ferment of activity in the Sixth Dwelling Places, the Seventh Dwelling Places are a space of fluidity, resolution and fruition. We see that the challenging growth that we have experienced over the course of our journey now bears fruit in an actual partnership with God, who has become the Friend who never leaves us and whose support and companionate presence allows us to draw strength and creativity from the "closeness" of God in all of our circumstances. The point of entry into this relational way of life is an experiential invitation into the life of the Trinity, which Teresa describes as an intellectual vision in whose consciousness she now lives. In other words, the life of the Trinity moves from being a perceived external truth to a living reality in which we participate. We are included in God's ongoing work of incarnating possibility in the world, as we live in and with the Love that gives life and is always stronger than death.

In outlining the seven dwelling places, I have tried to provide a sense of their intrinsic movement and progression, even as, in my own experience of them (and as Teresa herself always acknowledges), we are not always advancing. I will repeat

Teresa's sage observation, "Whoever does not grow, shrinks." Learning and integrating the lessons in each of the dwelling places is not enough to keep us from setbacks. We must live into the lessons and embody them relationally in our lives and in our world, and we must continually cultivate the relationship with God that provides daily guidance, clarity, consolation and inspiration.

While it may be possible to sustain and be sustained in the unitive life that Teresa describes in the seventh dwelling places, I think it far more likely that we will need to use the insights of various dwelling places to engage the challenges of life relationally with God, never afraid to begin again from wherever we are. The framework of *The Interior Castle* helps us recognize the health and quality of our relationship with God and the extent to which we have availed ourselves of all that God offers us. It also provides us with concrete ways to re-engage that relationship when we have gone astray, allowing us to return again to the One whom we know loves us.

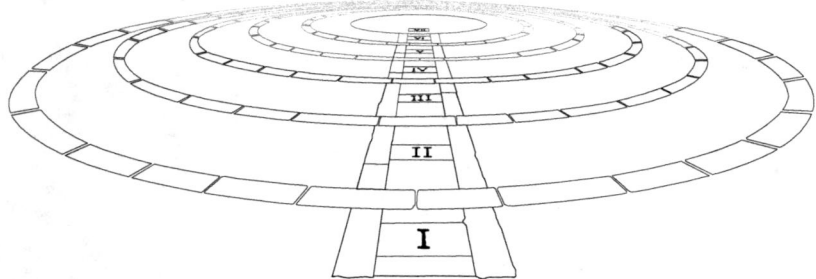

FIRST DWELLING PLACES

The First Dwelling Places are a space of consideration, where we pause to look around, at ourselves and our world, to reflect on who we are, who we've become, and whether or not we're growing in a way that supports and nurtures our inherent worth, dignity, and giftedness. As human beings we often do not know our own potential: we learn that potential, through experiences, good and bad, and we need help both to know who we can become and to grow toward our capacity for greatness. Not everything about being human is honorable or dignified; we can be cruel, contemptuous, lazy, deceitful, and even destructive and violent. Our company, our social norms, and our cultures can have strong impacts, often negative, on what we prioritize in our lives. As we take into account how often we've failed to live up to our potential, we should remind ourselves that, as human beings, we have limited perspectives and experiences. Additionally, our cognitive and emotional challenges (and all of us have them!) keep us from seeing or knowing everything. It is far better for us to acknowledge that there is much that we still have to learn.

We will advance further as we realize that we can never really know enough and we should always seek to understand, by listening, asking respectfully, and dedicating ourselves to learning from each experience life hands us. As a result of these considerations, we begin to sense that relationship with the divine, cultivated through honest, dialogical prayer, is critical to our growth as human beings.

Some of the habits that we can cultivate in the first dwelling places are:

- gratitude for the opportunity to live, to grow, to learn

- willingness to admit we are wrong or have made mistakes

- willingness to recognize behavioral patterns that must change if we are to grow

- willingness to recognize that alone, we are not enough and need a Higher Power

The First Dwelling Places with their metaphorical glimpses of the possibilities of the human person situate us at the beginning of an adventure—one that is not just an itinerary, but a way of life, a way of being a person, and a way of seeing, knowing and sharing life with God. Teresa shows us that the journey toward self-knowledge, authenticity, and agency as a human person is not simply a psychological project, but also an ethical one, a spiritual one, and a theological one. Indeed, these apparently singular pursuits are united in and through the medium of the self, so that what is learned in any of those arenas has profound implications for the others. What Teresa proposes is that, as we truly become ourselves, we are also participating in the ongoing creativity of God—allowing the divine to come alive, in us and in our world. Teresa generously shares with us her vision of and map for the unfolding of the divine-human partnership, and ignites a vision of potentiality that inspires us to change.

Gillian T.W. Ahlgren

A Place to Start:

Let us remember that within us
is a palace
of immense magnificence.

The Interior Castle rests on a central premise: we carry within us an unknown realm of unfathomable possibility, "a palace of immense magnificence." Entering into this inner world and fully dwelling in it, allowing its magnificence to change how we live in the world around us, is the project of our lives. It is the work of being human: the forging of an identity as children of God, as people of God who seek to make the world a place where God would feel at home.

Consider the following observations and journal about whether or not, in your experience, each one rings true. If that observation leads to further insight into your life, continue to explore it.

For as much as we have accomplished amazing things in our lives, whoever we are, we have not lived into the fullness of our potential. There is still more to discover about who we can become.

We may have wasted a lot of time and life energy in pursuits that have not led to our full self-realization.

Our efforts to construct an identity for ourselves must take into account not just who we think we are (or who others tell us we are) and what we think we want out of life, but also why we are here and who we can become.

An Initial Consideration

"Today, as I begged our Lord to speak for me because I wasn't able to think of anything to say nor did I even know how to begin to carry out this obedience, there came to my mind what I shall now speak about, so that we can begin on a solid foundation. It is that we consider our soul to be like a castle made entirely out of a diamond or very clear crystal, in which there are many rooms, just as in heaven there are many dwelling places. For if we consider it carefully, sisters, we see that the soul of the just person is nothing else but a paradise in which God finds delight. What kind of a place might it be where God—so powerful and wise, so pure and full of all good things—takes delight? I don't know if there is anything comparable to the magnificent beauty of a soul and its great capacity." (*Interior Castle* I:1:1)

"Well, let us consider that this castle has, as I said, many dwelling places: some up above, others down below, others to the sides; and in the center and middle of all of these is the main dwelling place where the very secret exchanges between God and the soul take place..." (*Interior Castle* I:1:3)

Take some time to imagine this castle and draw some representation of it, either in the form of a circle of rectangle, or, if you are more artistic, an actual castle. Include various dwelling places, perhaps with symbols and color, especially the "main dwelling place" in the center, acknowledging the divine presence there. Engage and explore this image for yourself in whatever way feels comfortable and spend time contemplating it when you finish.

Gillian T.W. Ahlgren

Reclaiming Our Souls

"It is no small pity and unfortunate that, through our own fault, we don't understand ourselves or know who we are. Wouldn't it show great ignorance, my daughters, if, when asked who we are, we could not name our own parents or even what country we come from? Well, if this would be ignorant of us, we are incomparably more lost in not striving to know who we really are, and in limiting ourselves to thinking that we are simply bodies walking this earth. We may have heard that we have souls. But we seldom consider what that means, what our capabilities are, who we can become, and, most importantly, Who dwells within us. This ignorance keeps us from cultivating our goodness and inner beauty, and we end up focusing our attention on the externals of life: our appearance and our place in society—nothing that matters before God." (*Interior Castle* I:1:2)

With this lament, Teresa wants to call our attention to the fundamental fallacy/dilemma/mistake of our lives: our lack of genuine self-knowledge keeps us from living in our identity as children of God. The work that Teresa calls us to attend to is to awaken to that identity, orienting ourselves towards God's indwelling presence and reclaiming our deepest dignity.

Thinking about your own self-image, consider some of the ways you have had a false understanding of who you are. Were there messages from your family of origin, your communities (past and present), your culture, or a friend/significant other that diminished you or otherwise distorted your self-image? Are there things that you can do to regain a greater sense of integrity?

Exercise: Creating Sacred Space

In this exercise you are invited to create a shrine or sacred space in your dwelling that enhances your prayer practice in some way. First, decide upon the space itself: which room? Corner? Wall? Table? Enclosed space? Inside a drawer or box? Then, decide how you might decorate it: Cloth? Images? Photos? Items from sacred moments or encounters? Symbols of lessons learned? How would you honor and commemorate the prayer of your life? Your love relationship with God? You may decide that you want more than one shrine in your home—or you may desire to slowly change your entire living space around that which is more conducive to your more constant recollection of all that supports the prayer of your life: think of things that recall for you the goodness of life, the blessings that you have received, the people who have inspired you or helped you to know God better.

If you already have such a place, take a deliberate moment to approach it with reverence, take in the objects that decorate it, remember what they symbolize, represent or commemorate, and consider whether or not you want to make any changes to it.

Gillian T.W. Ahlgren

Visiting the Room of Self-Knowledge

In the First Dwelling Places Teresa speaks of "visiting the room of self-knowledge" (I:1:8), and she encourages us to visit this room often. Even a soul who has reached the Seventh Dwelling Places never outgrows the benefits of visiting this room. The painful knowledge of our own inability to make best choices for ourselves, how petty, ungrateful, and small-minded we can be, or our failure to grow toward wisdom can become powerful motivating factors for us to turn to God more habitually.

Growing in self-knowledge is a life-long process. The exercises in this workbook will undoubtedly add to your self-understanding, but it will be helpful to spend some time at the outset gaining a clear, honest sense of where you are now. Use several or all of the following prompts to take stock of who and where you are, writing as much as you want. Use them periodically in order to continue your process of growth and adapt healthily to the needs of the world around you.

Some of my deepest strengths are...

If I had to name three areas in which I simply cannot compromise my beliefs or values, they would be...

I have been surprised when people have told me...

My life would be more satisfying to me if...

Something I have not yet been able to accomplish is...

I have been putting off...

An area of my life where I would like to grow is...

Take some time to reflect on what emerged from the above prompts. What do you notice? Share your observations with God and engage some kind of dialogical prayer in order to gain strength to change.

The Inner Garden

In *The Book of Her Life*, Teresa describes the soul as a garden space to be cultivated. She encourages all of us, especially beginners in prayer, to roll up our sleeves and make a garden in which God is to take delight, reminding us that we start with unfruitful soil full of weeds. Our work is to root out the weeds and ensure that the garden receives the water it needs so that flowers will grow—flowers like courage, character, kindness, integrity, concern for others, discretion, wisdom.

Take some time to imagine your inner garden. What would you consider its weeds that need to be uprooted? Are there habits (like avoidance, denial, numbing) that can get you into trouble? What would help you to do what you know would be good for your own growth? Fill in the space below with words and/or images representing the "weeds."

Now re-imagine your inner garden, filling it with all that leads to God's deepening life in you.

What virtues are already a part of who you are?

What graces do you need in order for your garden to flourish?

How will you make sure that the tiny seedlings get the nurturing they need?

Take some time to review the two spaces and pray for what you need in order to grow into your potential.

The Tree of Life

Another image of human potential that Teresa uses interchangeably with the interior castle is that of a "tree planted in the very living waters of life." (*Interior Castle* I:2:1). Using this image, draw a representation of yourself, flourishing. What is growing in the branches of your tree? Use words or images to show what your flourishing self can accomplish.

The Beauty and Majesty of God

Teresa's *Interior Castle* reflects her inherent appreciation of the beauty and majesty of God. Perhaps it is unwise to assume that all of us today have a similar consciousness of God's presence. Two avenues might provide helpful points of entry into a felt knowledge of God's presence: nature and an openness to friendship with the incarnate God.

How have you experienced the beauty of creation? Describe some moments in which you have been moved by the gift of nature.

Go for a slow walk in a natural setting and allow yourself to linger and notice the world around you. What do you do to maintain and enkindle your connection to creation? How can you engage greater care for creation?

We can also "picture ourselves in the presence of Christ... to speak with Christ, ask for what we need, complain of what is difficult for us, share our excitement and joy over things..." just as we would a closest friend. "This method of bringing Christ into our lives is helpful at all stages; it is a most certain means of making progress in the earliest stage, of quickly reaching the second degree of prayer." (See *Book of Her Life*, chapter 13)

Entering the Castle: Prayer

"Returning to our beautiful and delightful castle, now we must see how we can enter it. It may seem foolish for me to say that, since, if this castle is the soul, why would we need to enter it? How foolish it would be to tell people to enter a space where they already are! But you must understand that there are many ways to be, in this life—some might be in the outer courtyard with the guards and don't even want to go in; they won't appreciate all the mysteries in this precious place, nor who lives there, nor even how many rooms there are within us. You have already heard in some books on prayer that the soul is advised to enter within itself; well, that's the very thing I'm advising." (*Interior Castle* I:1:5)

"Insofar as I can understand, the gate of entry to this castle is prayer and reflection. I don't mean to refer to mental rather than vocal prayer, for since vocal prayer is prayer, it too must be accompanied by reflection. A prayer in which we are not aware of the One to whom we are praying, nor what we are asking, nor of Whom we are asking it, I do not call prayer, however much the lips may move." (*Interior Castle* I:1:7)

In these remarkably succinct paragraphs, Teresa extends to us an invitation to a journey and process, rooted in our relationship with the Author of life, that leads to deeper self-realization and fulfillment. For some of us, if we have little or no habit of prayer and are unsure of the existence of anything beyond this world, Teresa's invitation may fall on deaf ears. But this is a good time for us to reflect on our habits of prayer, using the following prompts:

How do you pray? When do you pray? How often do you pray?

What contexts and supports help deepen your prayer?

Do you leave time for listening within your practice of prayer?

How can you make more time for deeper prayer?

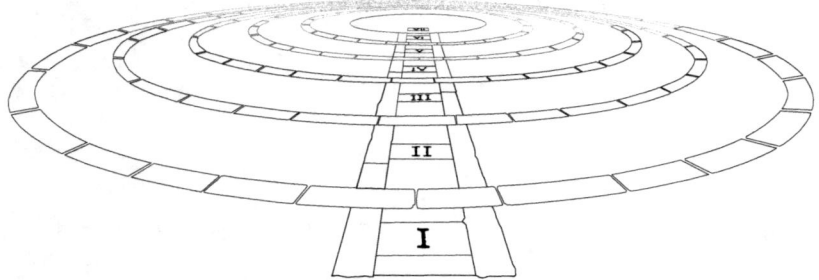

SECOND DWELLING PLACES

If we continue in the discipline of coming to know ourselves, entering more deeply into the Interior Castle, we proceed rather rapidly into the second dwelling places, where we begin to sense more deeply the invitation toward authenticity and a life in greater harmony with what God wants, for and with us. As Teresa describes it, "This stage describes those who have already begun to practice prayer and have understood how important it is not to stay in the first dwelling places…. So these persons are able to hear the Lord's callings." (*Interior Castle* I:1:2) Whether these "callings" are mediated through others, through life events, or experienced as a form of inner invitation to self-realization, in these second dwelling places we have a growing awareness of how God is inviting us into deeper life. We are challenged to consider how we will respond.

In the second dwelling places, we sense the call to a deeper, more godly way of life, and we desire to heed and respond to this call toward greater goodness. But it can be painful to see with greater clarity the many ways that entrenched habits keep us from doing what we know would be best for our relationship with God. In the Second Dwelling Places, we gain a humbling kind of self-knowledge, as we crash up against our limitations and realize how often we have put social success, professional accomplishment or even self-indulgence and numbing behaviors over genuine spiritual growth. The silver lining in this challenging wake-up call is the awareness of our radical need for grace, not only as a source of strength external to us (helping us to do what we cannot do by ourselves), but also as an orientation to goodness that works through and with us, awakened by the voice of God deep within.

If in the First Dwelling Places we became aware of our potential, in the Second Dwelling Places we understand how much effort it will take to realize our capacities. What carries the day in this conflict is the constancy of God's presence, which begins to instill us with greater power, as Teresa describes:

> "The will is inclined to love after seeing such countless demonstrations of love; now we want to repay something, especially as we consider how this true Lover never leaves us, accompanying us and giving us life and being. Then the intellect steps in, helping us realize that, as long as we might live, we cannot find a better friend; that the whole world is filled with falsehood; and that whatever pleasures the devil provides are filled with trials, cares, and contradictions." (*Interior Castle* II:1:4)

Desire

Our desires can get us into trouble, especially when we desire things that are either not good for our own well-being or not good for our relationship with God. However, without genuine desire, we are often unable to gain traction in our lives and summon the determination to accomplish hard things. In the Second Dwelling Places we begin to understand the inherent conflict in some of our desires, which are actively keeping us from greater contact and intimacy with God: we don't make time, we succumb to the "tyranny of the urgent," we are addicted to media feeds and other things that suck our energy and intellect...the list goes on and on. These are the "reptiles" that Teresa speaks of in the Second Dwelling Places, and until we confront them more actively, we could spend our entire lives chasing after them.

Many poets have written about human desire. If you would like a poetic framing for this reflection, I would recommend Rainer Maria Rilke's *Book of Hours: Love Poems to God* as translated by Anita Burrows and Joanna Macy. There is a poem that starts out "Du siehst, ich will viel...". ("You see: I want a lot...") Read the poem through several times, and consider a God who "takes pleasure in the faces of those who know they thirst" and "cherishes those who grip You for survival."

What do you really thirst and long for? Where do these longings come from?

Trace your longings down into their core, their center: what do you see there? (This may take several repeated times of considering and thinking, not only about what you truly long for but why.)

In what ways might your longings be resonant with God's?

Can you have a conversation with God about your longings?

Can you ask God to help you to see more clearly God's own longings?

How do your deepest desires align with the orientation and trajectory of your life so far?

Finding Spiritual Companions

"It's a wonderful thing for us to talk to those who are on a similar journey, to seek companions who are not only in the same rooms where we are but also those known to have entered the ones closer to the center. Conversation with them helps us tremendously, since they draw us nearer to where they are." (*Interior Castle* II:1:6)

As Teresa states above, it is always important to have people in our lives who are trustworthy companions, who can reliably help us to come to know ourselves better, and who can accompany us in a continual growth process that leads us to freedom and fulfillment of our deepest purpose. Such companions are even more important when we enter into new territories of growth and change. This exercise asks you to consider and engage these relationships more thoughtfully and deliberately.

Describe what you believe are the qualities of a spiritual companion or ally of your deepest self.

Who would you identify as those companions? How can you increase contact with them as you engage the exercises in this workbook?

List the personal qualities that you most value and most want to embody. Consider the contexts, relationships and supports that help you to embody those values. What conversations, with God, with yourself and with others, can you have that will help you to manifest the self you want to be? Make a list of conversational topics and create space for further dialogue with God, self and others over the next week.

Adversity: What Keeps Us from Self-Realization?

In the Second Dwelling Places, Teresa uses colorful language of lizards and snakes to refer to the many things that keep us from responding to the invitation of God to greater life. In II:1:3 she provides concrete examples of what some of these reptiles that keep us from God really are: "the esteem one has in the world, one's friends and relatives, one's health, and a thousand other obstacles." Thinking about the health of your relationship with God, what would you identify as the greatest barriers to God's deepening life in you?

Gillian T.W. Ahlgren

Two Columns

Following the still, small voice in our own depths probably requires changes in our daily habits and may even involve significant life changes—changing jobs, giving up career aspirations, severing relationships which become incompatible with the spiritual journey. A socially-defined self is often at odds with the self that is emerging from a knowledge of God within us. In the Second Dwelling Places we become more aware of how each and every life experience presents us with the opportunity to respond concretely to God; this places in sharp relief the ways in which our social patterns deny or preclude the possibility of that presence.

Review the two charts below, and fill them in first with behaviors and contexts which are compatible with your deepening relationship with God and second with those that are incompatible.

Tailor this list to the behaviors that you personally engage in and the situations you find yourself in.

Be sure to include social behaviors, cultural norms, and influences on you that correlate to the second chart below.

After you are finished, study what you have written and write about how you can begin to let go of what is incompatible with your deepening relationship with God.

These activities, people, approaches, places or times draw me toward God, help me to love more, help me want to be a better person:

Doing these things, being with these people or in these situations turns me away from my best self, makes me cynical, causes me to be blind to the presence of God:

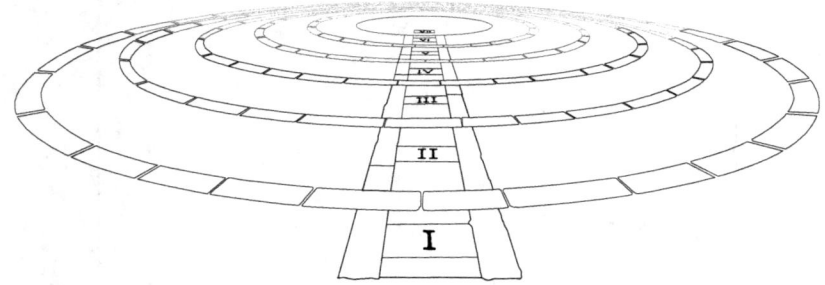

THIRD DWELLING PLACES

The Third Dwelling Places are a space of consolidation and transition. The biggest accomplishment that they represent is what Teresa calls "the union of wills," a space in which we have both the discipline and the grace to want what God wants. The inner conflicts and disordered responses to life that characterized the Second Dwelling Places are resolved here, since now we seek to please God in all things.

Interestingly, although the new moral groundedness is a help to our conscience, moral self-satisfaction can keep us in these dwelling places for the rest of our lives, without going any further. For a true union of wills is not about following a set of rules or principles, or even about aligning our own will with what we think is the will of God in a particular circumstance. Rather, moving beyond the Third Dwelling Places into the subsequent ones entails the kind of conscious choices one makes in a committed, loving relationship with a life-partner, actively striving toward realization of one's own and the other's fullness of being, in order to share the best of oneself with another. Reverence and love for God pulls us out of egocentricity, calling us into deeper relationship with God and others, changing us in the process.

The core question in the Third Dwelling Places, like the invitation extended to the "rich young man" in Matthew 19:16-22, is whether or not we will choose the adventure of relationship with God in all the ways that it will change us.

Fear of God?

"What shall we say to those who, through perseverance and the mercy of God have won the battles of the previous dwelling places and enter into these third rooms but: 'Blessed is the one who fears the Lord'?" (*Interior Castle* III:1:1)

How do you think Teresa understands the phrase from Psalm 112:1 "Blessed is the one who fears the Lord"? How do you experience awe and express reverence?

Consider and list the many things that you have to feel grateful for and joyful about. Be sure to dialogue with God after this reflection. Repeat this exercise daily through the week.

Choosing Love, Part 1

In *Interior Castle* III:2:1, Teresa describes a stumbling block for people in Third Dwelling Places who may have lived many years in a "righteous and well-ordered way": they are still easily perturbed by minor issues in life and "go about so disturbed and afflicted that it puzzles me…for they think that they are more than justified in feeling disturbed." In what follows, she gives spiritual counsel to such people, who "canonize their feelings in their minds and would like others to do so." (*Interior Castle* III:1:3)

To what extent are you bound up in the habit of self-righteousness?

Think about some of the times that you could not admit that you were wrong about something or had a limited, partial understanding of a situation, and your unwillingness to reconsider your position led to a problem with someone.

List some examples of when your own certainty about your perspective has gotten you into trouble or cost you something in terms of a relationship.

Have you ever "canonized your feelings" (of, for example, frustration, resentment, anger, shock, or grief) in your own mind and wanted validation from others that you were "right" in feeling a certain way? Looking back at a situation in which you did that, was there another way to understand that situation?

How might conversation with God change or broaden your perspective or help you to see that, while your feelings were valid, there was more to learn from the experience than you could learn when you were stuck in the depth of a particular feeling?

NOTE: In this consideration, it is wise to remember that there are times when compromising with others or with an organization or group actually compromises or even violates our integrity. Those situations would not be examples of the kind of self-righteousness Teresa encourages us to move beyond.

Walking Humbly with Our God

"If we turn our backs and go away sad, like the young man in the gospel when the Lord tells us what we must do to be perfect, what do you want God to do? For God rewards us according to our love for God. And this love, daughters, cannot be fabricated in our imagination; it must be proven in how we live and what we do. It's not so much about the works that we do; it's the determination of our wills that really matters." (*Interior Castle* III:1:7)

"This is what God asks of you, only this:

> To act justly,
> To love tenderly, and
> To walk humbly with your God."   (Micah 6:8)

Sit with the above quotes and read (or re-read) the exchange between Jesus and "the rich young man" in Matthew 19:16-22, along with the commentary in *Entering Teresa of Avila's Interior Castle: A Reader's Companion*, pp. 39-42.

Consider and list some of the ways that you can deepen the expression of your love for God and cultivate the loving dimensions of that relationship.

If God were to ask you directly to love more tenderly and to walk more humbly together with God through the rest of your life, what would need to change?

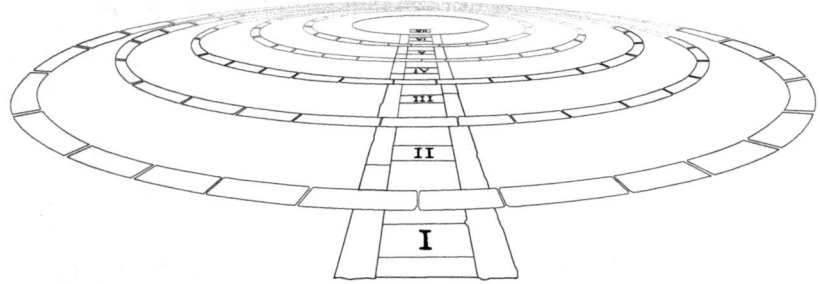

FOURTH DWELLING PLACES

The core scriptural text in the Fourth Dwelling Places is a line from the Psalms: "when you have expanded my heart." This phrase gives Teresa a point of departure to describe the ways that God's presence enlarges our being, lifting us out of petty small-mindedness and lack of generosity.

From the Fourth Dwelling Places onward, we must learn love from God. This becomes the focus of our prayer, our life, and our days, as we learn that everything that we do can be done lovingly; everything we think about can be thought about lovingly. As we dedicate ourselves to love as a constant way of being, we begin to learn how love has the capacity to change us. These are not lessons that we can teach ourselves! They are lessons we learn from the One who is Love loving us, and as we begin to learn them, the relational path through the subsequent Dwelling Places to that "central chamber" spoken of at the outset begins to unfold. It is a path made by walking a road less traveled, a movement toward what has not yet been realized in our natures as loving people.

Reflecting on Tenderness

The Fourth Dwelling Places represent a new phase in our relationship with God—one in which we are met with tenderness and experience the lovingkindness that is God. What do you know, from your experience, about tenderness?

Intuitively, where do you know that you need to be met with tenderness? Can you confide and commend that place to God?

How can you share the balm of tenderness with another person in need?

Gillian T.W. Ahlgren

Choosing Love, Part 2

In the Third Dwelling Places you considered how your own "righteous and well ordered" ways may have kept you from growing in empathy and comprehension of others' experiences of life. Now in the Fourth Dwelling Places Teresa's earlier insight that we can focus our energies and perspectives on the self or on our relationship with God and others deepens, as we choose more consciously to grow in love.

In the Fourth Dwelling Places our desire to know—particularly the intense questioning process of reason and the demand for logic and solutions—must be tempered by awe, resulting in the development of a patient openness to mystery. Here we learn the value of seeking not the most immediate answer, but a deeper way of living in and with questions. As we dedicate ourselves to a more integrated, affective way of knowing, we grow toward a more holistic way of being. As we choose to love more deeply, we allow love to order our daily lives, guiding us as we express compassion, empathy, and personal presence in the lives of others.

How can you bring love more consciously into the ways that you understand yourself, the world around you, and the people in your life? Make a list of these ways and begin to integrate them into daily life.

Identify two or three situations in your current life that would benefit from your focused empathy for another person. Holding those situations up to God in prayer, ask for the grace to be more empathetic, think of some ways that you can express greater empathy, and approach that person or those people to see what happens as you stay focused and grounded in your capacity to love them deeply.

Knowing the Consolation of God

Review some of the ways that God's presence has consoled you. Focus on a moment in which you felt that presence and spend time giving thanks for it.

"When You Have Enlarged My Heart…"

Review Teresa's description of the two fountains in chapter two of the Fourth Dwelling Places and, recalling that "however diligent our efforts we cannot acquire spiritual delights," pray quietly with the following passages:

> "You will ask me how then one can obtain them without seeking them… [T]he initial thing is to love God without self-interest." (*Interior Castle* IV:2:9)

> "In order to profit by this path and ascend to the dwelling places we desire, the important thing is not to think much but to love much; so do what best stirs you to love." (*Interior Castle* IV:1:7)

> "It is good to be aware of who God is and that one is in God's presence… Let the soul enjoy it without any endeavors other than some loving words." (*Interior Castle* IV:3:7)

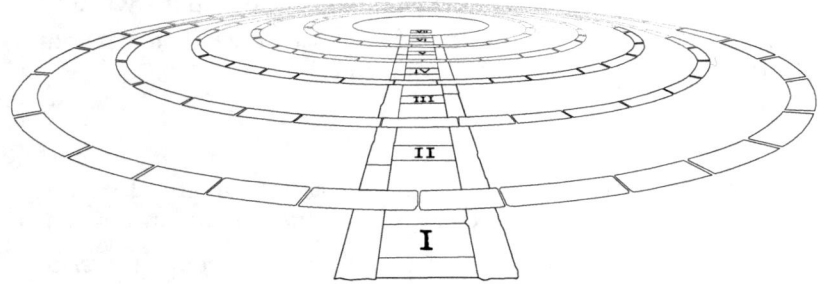

FIFTH DWELLING PLACES

The "expansion of the heart" in the Fourth Dwelling Places has not only shown us that we have a hidden and deep capacity to love; it has also prepared us to settle into new depths within us that God wants to share with us. Now the space created in us becomes the location for a powerful transformation that Teresa represents through a description of the metamorphosis of a caterpillar into a butterfly. For Teresa, the butterfly that emerges from the cocoon represents not just our new life in God, but also the transforming partnership with God that is still evolving.

As our encounters with God deepen and change us, we gain an experiential knowledge of how truly we are cherished and desired by a God who loves us into greater life. In the Fifth Dwelling Places the particularity of God's love for us is felt and known in lasting ways that strengthen us and forge life-long relational commitment in a way that resembles but surpasses sacramental love. These experiences communicate to us something of God's own being, of Love loving, and they attune us to God in ways that absorb us with their intensity. Teresa's use of Matthew 22:14 ("Many are called but few are chosen") provides a point of entry into the particularity and profundity of these experiences of God.

Reflecting on Chosenness

"Although many are called, few are chosen..." (*Interior Castle*, V:1:2)

What is it to be "chosen," and can that adjective help us frame a new identity rooted in the depths of our relationship with God? That is the central question that Teresa poses us, and she asks us, at this stage, not just to consider such a possibility, but to embrace it.

The challenge of this task is addressed in a beautiful portion of Henri Nouwen's *Life of the Beloved*, which could serve as reflective reading at the outset of our journey into the Fifth Dwelling Places. "I beg you," Nouwen writes to a friend, "do not surrender the word 'chosen;' dare to claim it as your own... That truth is the bedrock on which you can build a life as God's beloved." (Henri Nouwen, *Life of the Beloved*, p. 52. Read the entire chapter entitled "Taken" if you would like to explore how Nouwen develops the idea of our chosenness.)

One of the more basic ways that we can begin to appropriate this identity as God's chosen is to receive from God what God wants to give us. The central paradigm shift is not so much one of "surrendering" to God as to turning to God with the greatest of openness, setting down the typical "tools" of prayer and allowing ourselves to *be fed from God*, through time alone with God in prayer. While "being fed" from God is clearly not something we can control, we can certainly dispose ourselves to giving God the entirety of our attention and our being, and rejoicing as we come to know more completely the bounty and generosity of this good God of ours. Explore this notion of being fed by God in prayer.

Gillian T.W. Ahlgren

Digging for the Hidden Treasure

Appropriating an identity in which we see and know ourselves for who we most deeply are requires us to see ourselves as something more than what life has made of us. Thankfully, we are more than the sum total of our life experiences, many of which may easily have formed us toward becoming something other than our deepest potential. To claim the reality that we are "chosen" and "beloved" is to see ourselves as someone who is both contained by and yet transcends the life narrative that we might relate to another person. It is to see ourselves as the child of God whom God wants to grow into a gracious person of wisdom and goodness. In the fifth dwelling places, Teresa writes:

"We walk in the footsteps of others who have heard this call and sought out the treasure of contemplation that we are speaking about. Yet few of us open ourselves to the ways that God reveals this treasure to us. From the outside we may appear to be proceeding well; but in the practice of the virtues that are necessary for arriving at this point we cannot be careless in either small or large matters. So, my sisters, since in some way we can enjoy heaven on earth, be brave in begging God to grace us with all that we need, so that nothing will be lacking through our own fault; and that God will show us the way and strengthen us in our digging until we find this hidden treasure. The truth is that the treasure lies within our very selves." (*Interior Castle* V:1:2)

For some of us, this "digging"—or foraging for a deeper identity—involves uncovering the person who is beneath and beyond the experiences of our lives that have taxed and troubled us. It means finding the threads of continuity and growth that, despite trauma and disruption, can still be woven together into a tapestry of meaning and intrinsic beauty. Perhaps this is one way to approach the work of the caterpillar that Teresa describes in chapter two of these Fifth Dwelling Places:

> The silkworms nourish themselves on the mulberry leaves until, having grown to full size, they settle on some twigs, and there, with their little mouths, they themselves go about spinning the silk and making some very thick little cocoons in which they enclose themselves. The silkworm, which is fat and ugly, then dies, and a little white butterfly, which is very pretty, comes forth from the cocoon. (*Interior Castle* V:2:2)

Spend some time reviewing your life for the threads of integrity and goodness that have helped you reach this point in your life. Give thanks for being here. Ask God to help you to see whatever wholeness is an intrinsic part of your life. Let go of preconceived ideas about what your life "should" look like and ask God to help you to see your own beauty.

Reflecting on Union with God

The Fifth Dwelling Places are a space in which God joins Godself with us in such an absorbing way that we lack awareness of anything else. Here is how Teresa describes our absorption in God, at this stage:

> "There is neither imagination, nor memory, nor intellect that can impede this good. This union is above all earthly joys, above all delights, above all consolations, and still more than that. It doesn't matter where those spiritual or earthly joys come from, for the feeling is very different, as you will have experienced. I once said that the difference is like that between feeling something on the rough outer covering of the body or in the marrow of the bones. And that was right on the mark, for I don't know how to say it better." (*Interior Castle* V:1:5)

Have you ever had an experience of absorption in something? Think about that moment, and, if you have never had an experience of absorption in God, imagine what absorption in God might be like, based on what you *have* experienced. Because we cannot bring about such experiences of absorption, focus on what you can do to prepare yourself for them and be ready for them, should they come.

The Life That Is Hidden in God

Teresa likens what we can do to prepare ourselves for this kind of union with God to the work of the caterpillar in preparing the cocoon. Review chapter two of the Fifth Dwelling Places and consider in particular this paragraph:

"Well, once this silkworm is grown, it begins to spin the silk and build the house wherein it will die. I would like to point out here that this house is Christ. Somewhere, it seems to me, I have read or heard that our life is hidden in Christ or in God (both are the same), or that our life is Christ. [see Colossians 3:3-4] Whether the quotation is exact or not doesn't matter for what I intend. Well, see here, daughters, what we can do through the help of God: God becomes the dwelling place we build for ourselves." (*Interior Castle* V:2:4)

Gillian T.W. Ahlgren

What We Can Do

Because there is so much in the Fifth Dwelling Places that we ourselves cannot control, our focus has to be on the area where we can always improve: love of neighbor. Review the two passages below:

"I have said a lot on this subject elsewhere, because I see, Sisters, that if we fail in love of neighbor we are lost. Please God that this will never be so; for if you do not fail, I tell you that you shall receive from God the union that was mentioned. When you see yourselves lacking in this love, even though you have devotion and gratifying experiences that make you think you have reached this stage, and you experience some little suspension in the prayer of quiet (for to some it then appears that everything has been accomplished), believe me, you have not reached union. Instead, beg our Lord to give you this perfect love of neighbor. Let God do what you cannot, for God will give you more than you even know how to desire, especially when you are striving and making every effort to grow in love." (*Interior Castle* V:3:12)

"Let this, in sum, be the conclusion: that we strive always to advance. And if we cannot, let us walk with great care. Without doubt the devil wants to see us lapse and backpedal, but it ought not be possible that, after having come so far, one would fail to grow. Love is never idle, and laziness in love would be a very bad sign. A soul that is called to be betrothed with the living God and is now intimate with God, having reached what I've described, must not fall asleep." (*Interior Castle* V:4:10)

Make a list of the concrete commitments to spiritual advancement and love of others that you can implement and begin to incorporate them in your daily life. Remember, too, that we can always pray for deepest integrity and fidelity, even when we do not know concretely where and how to grow in our integrity and fidelity. Incorporate that prayer into your daily practice.

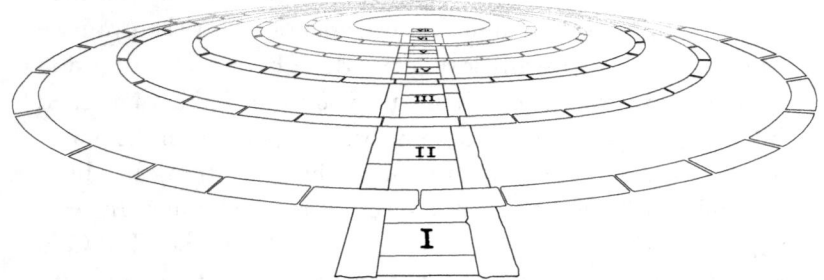

SIXTH DWELLING PLACES

The Sixth Dwelling Places are the most complex and dense of the stages of transformative growth. There are eleven chapters in this section of *The Interior Castle*, and, in length, the Sixth Dwelling Places are nearly as long as the entire remainder of the book. In these chapters, Teresa presents readers with a rich catalog of ways that God communicates directly with us—through words given to us, images, insights, and a sense of felt presence. Teresa's own experiences inform her descriptions, of course, and she does not assume that readers will have the same experiences she did. She *is* concerned, however, that female readers of her text who *do* have some of the experiences described in this section will likely receive the same kind of doubt and even scorn from their confessors that Teresa herself did. Her intent is, then, to empower readers to recognize some of the ways that they may experience God directly.

Practicing Solitude

"Well then, let us, with the help of the Holy Spirit, speak of the sixth dwelling places, where the soul is now wounded with love for its Spouse and strives for more opportunities to be alone and rid itself of everything, in conformity with its state, that might be an obstacle to this solitude." (*Interior Castle* VI:1:1)

As we move through some of the complex material in the Sixth Dwelling Places, continue to recall the above framing of this spiritual space: we seek solitude as a space of refuge, comfort, and intimacy with God. Prioritize this space for sacred encounter by creating more time and space in your daily life for prayer. Identify remaining "obstacles to solitude" and rid yourself of some of them.

The Wound of Love

Now re-read Teresa's introduction to the Sixth Dwelling Places, focusing on what this "wound of love" might be:

"Well then, let us, with the help of the Holy Spirit, speak of the sixth dwelling places, where the soul is now wounded with love for its Spouse and strives for more opportunities to be alone and rid itself of everything, in conformity with its state, that might be an obstacle to this solitude." (VI:1:1)

While Teresa's reference to being "wounded with love" may sound dramatic and even a bit extreme to modern readers, this language has a long history within Christian spirituality, going back to how the Song of Songs was understood to describe not just the love between two human beings but also the love between the soul and God. Specifically, it is a reference to Song of Songs 5:8, where the dialogue between two lovers moves to a place where the bride says she is "sick with love" for the groom. How are we to understand this language? If we recall how Teresa describes the "well-ordered person" in the Third Dwelling Places, where "love has not yet reached the point of overwhelming reason," we see how keenly attuned the soul has become to the loving presence of God. The wound represents both our sensitivity to God and our completely open disposition to God's communication to us. Spend some time pondering this wound of love and praying for it. You might refer to *Entering Teresa of Avila's Interior Castle: A Reader's Companion*, pp. 79-88 for further description of this state.

The Struggle for Serenity

New challenges beset us in these Sixth Dwelling Places. Teresa describes these challenges in detail, and they have several sources. The first category of challenges includes the doubts or even disparagement of others, who do not support or understand our spiritual aspirations. Their scorn can sting and perhaps cause self-doubt. The second category of challenges is an inner aridity: we come to an interior space in which we derive little to no consolation from our spiritual practices, and there is little to nothing that we can do to make further progress. This, too, can bring self-doubt. Another series of challenges may come from those who regularly serve as our mentors or even spiritual directors, but whose scrutiny or criticism or lack of insight increases our self-doubt. Read chapter one carefully for descriptions of these challenges, and do a new inventory to see if any of your current struggles correspond to the categories Teresa outlines. Pray with Teresa's counsel in VI:1:10: "In sum, there is no remedy in this tempest but to wait for the mercy of God. For at an unexpected time, with one word alone or even a chance happening, God so quickly calms the storm that it seems that there had not been even as much as a cloud in that soul, and it is left full of light and great consolation." Remember that serenity is a gift of the Spirit and ask for it, trusting that it will come in its own time.

Forms of Spiritual Communication

Much of the material in chapters two through four of the Sixth Dwelling Places describes forms of communication from God that we might experience at this stage. Recall that Teresa states very clearly throughout *The Interior Castle* that these phenomena are not something we should seek or ask for. Rather, she is describing experiences that some of her readers may have had and which would have been met with deep suspicion by some spiritual directors during Teresa's time.

Review this material to see if you can summarize the phenomena that Teresa is describing—for example, what a locution is and how you would identify one. Thinking back through your own experiences of God, does any of Teresa's language help you to understand your experiences better? For example, have you ever received a word or phrase in prayer that remains embedded in your heart? Do you have a memory of God that seems imprinted in your psyche?

Intellectual Visions and Compassionate Presence

The material in chapters eight through twelve, in which Teresa describes visions and apparitions, is dense and varied. Since these are experiences that are given to us rather than something we can generate, there are not exercises that correlate to the material. However, a deep reading of this material can shed light on experiences of God's companionate presence that we might sometimes sense in prayer. Consider, for example, Teresa's description in VI:8:2:

> "It will happen while the soul is heedless of any thought about such a favor being granted to it... that it will feel Jesus Christ, our Lord, beside it."

Teresa clarifies that this is not a case of actually seeing Jesus but rather an experience that helps us "walk with a habitual remembrance of God and a deep concern about avoiding anything displeasing to God," since we have an acute awareness of God's closeness and capacity to see all that we do. She also says that this is a "delicate" experience that "brings interior benefits" including greater "purity of conscience" as our desire to please God in all things increases. (See *Interior Castle* VI:8:3-4.)

While this kind of experience is clearly outside of our capacity to bring about, it is not impossible to take time to consciously imagine what it would be like to walk in the conscious presence of Jesus. In fact, if we were to add to our prayer time an extended moment of "continual companionship" with God in prayer, we might have a greater sense of what Teresa describes in VI:8:4:

"For even though we already know that God is present in all we do, our nature is such that we neglect to think of this. Here the truth cannot be forgotten, for the Lord awakens the soul to the divine presence beside it... [T]he soul goes about almost continually with actual love for the One who it sees and understands is at its side."

If we were able to increase our actual love for God in any measurable way through this act of imagining God at our side, we ought not hesitate to give such a thing a try. Spend some time integrating this moment of companionate presence into your prayer times and see what happens.

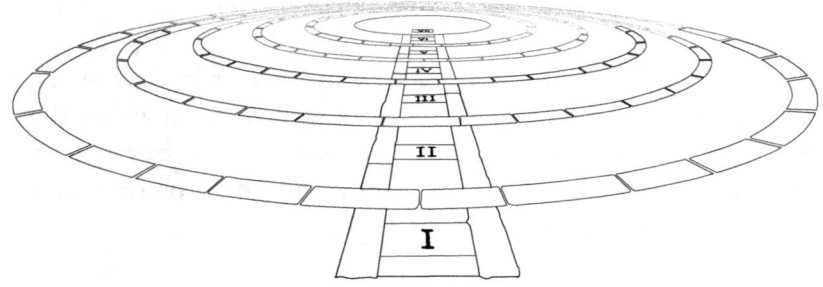

SEVENTH DWELLING PLACES

Although Teresa's descriptions of encounters with God up to this point have led us to believe that, if and when we reach union with God, it will be a union with God or with Christ, we are surprised, in this Seventh Dwelling Places, that Teresa's characterization of the unitive life suggests that it is dynamic and multi-faceted. Rather than being a space of "rest," life with God in the Seventh Dwelling Places is the fruition of a living, creative partnership. We are invited to participate in the life of the Trinity, with its effervescent love filling us with the grace and courage necessary to collaborate, with God, in the work of incarnating love in a messy, hurting world.

Living with Grace and Generosity

If we are brought into the Seventh Dwelling Places, it will not be either because of our merit or our efforts; it will be an expression of the abundant generosity of the God of life and love. Any "exercises" here will of necessity center around supporting our capacity to sustain both the presence and the activity of the One who loves the world into greater possibility. One element of our work in these dwelling places is to ensure that our lives (what we do, what we consider and how we consider it, how we spend each moment) are lived from the wellspring of God's generosity. We may need to reinforce our experiential knowledge of God with continual reflections on God's abundant generosity.

As you now know, Teresa is the perfect companion in this reflection! Her life-long commitment to invite people into a deeper, more genuine, more life-giving, and more challenging relationship with God respected the reality that the course of each person's trajectory toward the divine is unique and is ultimately forged within the space of intimacy between God and each person. Yet she also realized that, until and unless supported, we can often get stalled on the way to partnership with God because we do not always know how to deepen our response to the God of our lives.

Read through Teresa's observations about God, sprinkled throughout the Sixth and Seventh Dwelling Places, and copy a few onto a piece of paper. Meditate with them, considering the consistency and creativity of God's love. Imagine that love spilling over you, through you, and out of you, gracing you with the constant possibility of collaboration with Love in the work of Love throughout the world.

Gillian T.W. Ahlgren

Spend time in silent gratitude for God's constant loving activity, God's generosity, God's desire to share life with us, God's desire to dwell and live within us and empower us in goodness and wisdom and care.

Ask for the grace to be given deeper awareness of God's love and to be taught directly from God what Love truly is.

Protecting Relational Space with God

The metaphors Teresa has used throughout the Interior Castle—the castle itself with its walls, the turtle tucked into its shell, the caterpillar safely in its cocoon—suggest that our life-with-God needs a certain amount of insulation and protection from the forces in the world that surround us, can distract us or assault our sensitivities and numb us, even when we now know the divine life that wants to spill out, through us, into the hurting and needy world. Now that you know the competing pulls and energies of living with God in this world, what can you do to engage the world wisely and in ways that will not disrupt the growth you have experienced and the We (God and I) that is being born in you?

List some commitments you can make to We-time with God and some *new* habits that will help you continue to make progress toward your partnership with God.

Reflecting on Collaboration with God

Have you ever been empowered to do something that you alone knew that you could not do? How did that work? Have you ever been a part of a community in which you felt strongly the energy of God in your midst, empowering you to do something extraordinary? How did that work? Go back into one of those times of your life in order to remember carefully and consider all of the details of the process of empowerment. (If you cannot think of one in your own life, interview someone who did something you consider quite extraordinary and ask them what the process was like.) Can you recognize the presence of God in that process? In what senses was God *collaborating* with you or, better, were you and God collaborating in that process?

If this was possible in your own past or in someone else's, how might it be possible for you going forward? Spend some time with God considering this possibility Together.

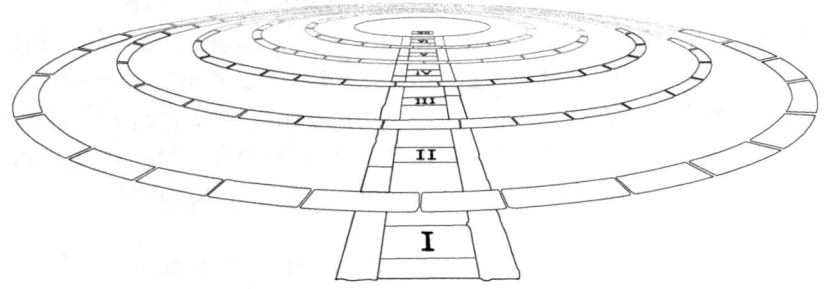

Committing Yourself to Ongoing Growth

"I repeat, it is necessary that your foundation consist of more than prayer and contemplation. If you do not strive for the virtues and practice them continually, you will always be dwarfs. And, please God, it will be only a matter of not growing, for you already know that whoever does not grow shrinks. I hold that love, where present, cannot possibly be content with remaining always the same." (*Interior Castle* VII:4:9)

"This is what I want, my sisters, for us to try to achieve: let us desire and occupy ourselves in prayer—not for the sake of our enjoyment but so as to have this strength to serve. Let's not want to go by way of an unknown path, which would be a waste of time, especially if we were to expect favors from God through a path other than the one that Christ took or the saints who follow. May such a thought never enter our minds. Believe me, Martha and Mary must join together in order to show hospitality to God, and be in God's presence as thoughtful hosts, not failing to provide something to eat. How would Mary, always seated nearby, provide food if her sister did not help her? God's food is that in every way possible we draw souls that they may be saved and absorbed in the love and praise of God always... This fire of love in you enkindles their souls, and with every other virtue you will be always awakening them." (*Interior Castle* VII: 4:12,14)

What Teresa makes clear in the above paragraphs is that our self-realization must be integrated with (and, indeed, is dependent upon) our generous orientation to the needs of others around us. Thinking about your experience of this workbook and the insights you gained, what did you learn about yourself, about God, about the world, and about your purpose?

What do you still want to learn, understand, and experience in order to keep growing?

Reflecting on your own talents, passions, and interests, how can they be more deeply vectored toward contributing to a better world? Are there ways of deepening your engagement with the voiceless and creating hope for those left behind? What communal resources do you have that will help you sustain your passion to contribute to a better world?

What changes to your daily routine are important to support your ongoing life with God? How will you be both Mary and Martha?

Some Resources for Further Reading

Recommended version of Teresa's *Interior Castle*:

Kieran Kavanaugh and Otilio Rodriguez, *The Interior Castle: Study Edition*. Institute of Carmelite Studies, 2020.

Biographies and Studies on Teresa:

Gillian T. W. Ahlgren, *Teresa of Avila and the Politics of Sanctity*. Cornell University Press, 1996.

J. Mary Luti, *Teresa of Avila's Way*. Liturgical Press, 1991.

Barbara Mujica, *Teresa of Avila: Lettered Woman*, Vanderbilt University Press, 2009.

Peter Tyler and Eddie Howells, eds., *Teresa of Avila: Mystical Theology and Spirituality in the Carmelite Tradition*, Routledge, 2016.

Alison Weber, *Teresa of Avila and the Rhetoric of Femininity*. Princeton University Press, 1990.

Rowan Williams, *Teresa of Avila*, Bloomsbury, 2004.

Commentaries on *The Interior Castle* or Teresian Prayer:

Gillian T. W. Ahlgren, *Entering Teresa of Avila's Interior Castle: A Reader's Companion.* Paulist Press, 2005

Other Resources:

Henri Nouwen, *Life of the Beloved: Spiritual Living in a Secular World*, Crossroad, 2002.

Rainer Maria Rilke, *Rilke's Book of Hours: Love Letters to God* (trans. Anita Burrows and Joanna Macy), Riverhead Books, 1997.

About the Author

Gillian T. W. Ahlgren is Professor Emerita of Theology at Xavier University, where she began teaching in 1990. She received her Ph.D. from the University of Chicago in the History of Christianity with a specialization in the Christian mystical tradition. In addition to teaching graduate and undergraduate courses in theology, the history of Christianity, and Christian spirituality, she designs and facilitates retreats and immersive experiences that support personal and social transformation.

Palace Within is her eighth book. Her previous books include *Teresa of Avila and the Politics of Sanctity* (Cornell University Press, 1996), *Entering Teresa of Avila's Interior Castle: A Reader's Companion* (Paulist Press, 2005), *The Inquisition of Francisca: A Sixteenth-Century Visionary on Trial* (University of Chicago Press, 2005), *Enkindling Love: The Legacy of Teresa of Avila and John of the Cross* (Fortress Press, 2016), *The Tenderness of God: Reclaiming Our Humanity* (Fortress Press, 2017) and *Spiritual Exercises for the 21st Century: A Workbook* (third edition VITALITY, 2025). Dr. Ahlgren is internationally known for her work on Teresa and regularly gives public lectures and workshops on Teresian spirituality and *The Interior Castle* more specifically.

In addition to her work as a scholar and teacher, Dr. Ahlgren has been engaged in pastoral work at a variety of levels. After training in spiritual direction at the Center for Religious Development in 2005, she began to design and facilitate retreats, especially with those at the margins. In 2009 she was a founding member of the Cincinnati Women's Team of the Ignatian Spirituality Project, a national organization providing spiritual accompaniment for formerly homeless women in recovery from substance abuse. Since 2013 she has used Teresa's *Interior Castle* in her work with women who have survived domestic violence. In 2015, on the occasion of the 500th anniversary of Teresa's birth, she gave multiple lectures and keynote addresses in the United States and abroad. She periodically offers a week-long Spiritual Immersion Experience in the Footsteps of Teresa in Avila, in which participants go through *The Interior Castle,* day by day *in situ.*

Dr. Ahlgren is available to facilitate workshops, training programs, immersions, and retreats. Please contact her at ahlgren@xavier.edu.

About Resources for Renewal

Resources for Renewal is an educational 501(c)3 offering programming in renewal, reflection, immersion and discernment. Using tools from the Christian mystical tradition, we promote greater access to human resilience using insights from spiritual leaders and contemplative practices. We seek to support strong leaders and to nurture the strength of communities, so that the work of discernment, stewardship, and pastoral accompaniment is shouldered together, and so that all can participate in and share the joys of growth and human fruition. We provide onsite workshops and retreats and offer Spiritual Immersion Experiences in Assisi, Avila, and Montserrat.

Gillian T.W. Ahlgren

About VITALITY

VITALITY is a circle of friends welcoming all, awakening each other, and reminding each other that we are Whole. Our affordable self-care programs invite everyone to move, to breathe, to rest, to contemplate, to grow...wherever each person begins their self-care journey, wherever and however they want to become.

It's the power of a circle!

We invite you to explore with us through our

donation-based classes...in person & via Zoom
affordable trainings
individual sessions
volunteer opportunities

vitalitycincinnati.org

VITALITY
buzz, bliss + books

publishing books from VITALITY's circle of friends
inspiring love, creativity, + possibility

vitalitybuzz.org

www.ingramcontent.com/pod-product-compliance
Lightning Source LLC
Chambersburg PA
CBHW071024120626
46546CB00003B/1209